Antone De Beelen Mackenzie

History of the Gazzam Family

Antone De Beelen Mackenzie

History of the Gazzam Family

ISBN/EAN: 9783337074142

Printed in Europe, USA, Canada, Australia, Japan

Cover: Foto ©ninafisch / pixelio.de

More available books at **www.hansebooks.com**

HISTORY

OF THE

GAZZAM FAMILY,

TOGETHER WITH A BIOGRAPHICAL SKETCH OF THE AMERICAN
BRANCH OF THE FAMILY OF

DeBEELEN,

BY

A. DeB. MACKENZIE.

PRINTED FOR PRIVATE CIRCULATION BY CHARLES F. HAAGE,
READING, PA.

THE GAZZAM FAMILY.

The earliest accurate knowledge of the present Gazzam family relates to William Gazzam, who lived in Cambridge, England, during the middle of the eighteenth century.

The name itself, however, is an extremely old one, mention of it being made in the Bible (Ezra ii, 48, and Nehemiah vii, 51). It is supposed to be of Egyptian origin, as records are extant in which a province or district bearing the name is mentioned. It may well be that the present members of the family are really lineal descendants of Abraham, through the ancient hewers of wood and drawers of water who bore the name when the Prophets returned with the "Remnant" to rebuild the Temple. The ancient Gazzams were called "Nethenims," or servants of Solomon and the Temple. Their chief city was Gibeon, and they traced their origin to a grandson of Noah, being recorded among the Hivites. One Biblical record has the name spelled Gazera, by mistake.

(1) WILLIAM GAZZAM.

Little is known of William Gazzam, the common ancestor of the American and English branches of the Gazzam family, beyond the fact that he married Martha Hart,* daughter of Joseph Hart, of Burwell, Cambridgeshire, England ; that he was the father of eight children, and

*See plate.

that his wife was many years a widow, dying during a
visit her youngest daughter, (*9*) Mrs. Mary Alice Gazzam-
Taylor, made to England in 1796 or 1797. One other fact
is also known, that the couple were highly-respected
people and devout Christians, as is shown by a letter Mrs.
Taylor wrote to her sisters in America. In this she said :—

"Some of the sentences spoken by our dear mother, before her departure hence, were these : 'Lord, make them willing in the day of
Thy power.' 'He is the same yesterday, to-day, and forever; not only
here, but in America also." [Alluding to her children there.] "He will
be my surety." 'He undertook my cause for me.' 'Be ye also ready.
* * * But tell them it must be through Christ Jesus, not measured by
their work, but by His grace through faith in Him.' 'My God and my
God, be Thou my shield and my defense.' 'Oh! tell them to pray ; to
teach their children.' 'O Lord ! remember them in the day when Thou
makest up Thy jewels.' "

Of the children of (*1*) William Gazzam, the five daugh-
ters, and their husbands and one son, (*5*) William, and his
wife came to America, leaving but one child in England,
(*7*) Joseph, who subsequently married Ann Goodcheap.

The name Gazzam is believed to be extinct in England.

THE CHILDREN OF (*1*) WILLIAM AND MARTHA GAZZAM.

The names of the children of William and Martha Gazzam, together with the known time of their births and
deaths, are as follows :—

(*2*) *Martha ;* born April 25, 1755; married William Girlling, of St. Giles' Parish, Cambridge, September 3, 1781,
at Great St. Mary's, Cambridge, England. There is no
known record of the year of their removal to America.
Mrs. Girlling died August 19, 1813, at Philadelphia, Pa.,
and is buried at Germantown, Pa., in the Presbyterian

[From a picture in the possession of J. B. Gazzam, St. Louis, Mo. The original picture having been damaged by fire, the hood was painted upon it by an amateur artist.]

MRS. MARTHA HART-GAZZAM.

(See page 1.)

Burial Ground, Lots, 74 and 75. Mr. Girlling died April 14, 1839, at Bustleton, Pa. Of this marriage there was issue six children. (*See post, Nos. 10–15.*)

(*3*) *Mary;* born March 14, 1757; married William Chilcott Larwill, March 20, 1782, at Great St. Mary's, Cambridge, England. Mrs. Larwill died March 17, 1827, at Wooster, Ohio, aged 70 years and 3 days. Mr. Larwill died November 12, 1832, at Wheeling, West Va., aged 81 years, 6 months, 4 days. Of this marriage there was issue nine children. (*See post, Nos. 16–24.*)

(*4*) *Sarah;* died in England of consumption, aged 18 years.

(*5*)* *William;* born in 1763 ; died November 16, 1811. He was twice married, and the father of sixteen children. (*See post, Nos. 25–40.*

(*6*) *Lydia;* born in Cambridge, England, in 1767 ; married David Kimpton in England, and removed with her husband to America, residing in Carlisle, Pa. They removed to Beulah, Pa., and thence, in 1809 or 1810, to a farm in Wayne County, Ohio, where Mrs. Kimpton died April 8, 1827. Mr. Kimpton preached in the first house of worship (Baptist) erected in Wayne County, Ohio. He died near Newark, Ohio. Of this marriage there was issue nine children. (*See post, Nos. 41–49.*)

(*7*) *Joseph;* married Ann Goodcheap, in England, October 19, 1795. The date of his death is not known. He was living in 1827, and also his daughter, (*54*) Susannah, who lived at Burwell with her Aunt Goodcheap. Joseph Gazzam at one time lived at No. 19 Ivy Lane, Newgate Street, London, England. At last accounts there was but one daughter living, of whom all trace has been lost. Of the marriage of Joseph and Ann Goodcheap Gazzam there was issue seven children. (*See post, Nos. 50-56.*)

(*8*) **Rebecca;* born in Cambridge, England, 1770 or 1771 ; died in Baltimore, Md, January 1, 1813 ; married, at Philadelphia, Pa., Edward Jones, of Wales [born January 18, 1767], who came over on the same ship with her from England. Rebecca came over to have charge of the motherless children of her brother, (*5*) William. Mr. Jones died at Mobile, Ala., December 25, 1838. Of this marriage there was issue seven children. (*See post, Nos. 57-63.*)

(*9*) *Mary Alice;* born at Cambridge, England, June 11, 1774 ; died at Greenbush, N. Y., August 11, 1831. She was married at the Church of the Great St. Mary, Cambridge, England, February 20, 1794, to William Taylor, Jr., a son of William Taylor, of Cambridge. Mr. Taylor, Sr., came to this country in 1794, with his wife and son, William. He is reputed to have been possessed of considerable means. He first went to New Castle, Del., and thence to Philadelphia, where he purchased land and built a handsome residence, in which he lived until his death in 1822, at the age of 88 years. William Taylor the younger was born at Cambridge, England, June 11, 1772; and died at the residence of his son, (*67*) Dr. Benjamin C. Taylor, Bergen, Hudson County, N. J., April 9, 1849. He was an importing merchant in Philadelphia, being associated with Messrs. William Gazzam and Edward Jones,† and subsequently with William Sheepshanks, William Shufflebotton, James Curran and Gilbert Gay. Of his marriage with Mary Alice Gazzam there was issue eleven children. (*See post, Nos. 64-74.*)

---

*See plate. †See biographic sketch of (*5*) William Gazzam, post.

THE CHILDREN AND GRANDCHILDREN OF WILLIAM AND (2) MARTHA GAZZAM-GIRLLING.

(*10*) *Martha Maria ;* died May 20, 1808.

(*11*) *Elizabeth ;* died October 13, 1820.

(*12*) *Sarah ;* died February 23, 1818, at Philadelphia, Pa. ; married, at Philadelphia, Thomas Watson, March 5, 1812. Of this marriage there was issue three children :—

> (*75*) *William Lansdell ;* born January 13, 1813 ; died at Bridgeport, Conn., October 13, 1867.
>
> (*76*) *James ;* born and died July 15, 1815.
>
> (*77*) *George Robinson ;* born September 29, 1816 ; died at Wooster, Ohio, July 5, 1821.

(*13*) *Rebecca ;* died at Newark, Ohio, February 17, 1865.

(*14*) *Mary ;* died September 2, 1829.

(*15*) *Thomas Lansdell ;* born 1796 ; died at Wooster, Ohio, April 9, 1826, aged 31 years ; married Mary Quinby, at Warren, Ohio, July 22, 1823. Of this marriage there was issue one child :—

> (*78*) *William ;* died at Wooster, O., in 1825 or 1826.

Mrs. Mary Quinby-Girlling married a second time Dr. S. Spellman, of Granville, Ohio, and died at Wooster, Ohio, April 24, 1888, aged 86 years, 3 months, 12 days.

———

THE CHILDREN AND GRANDCHILDREN OF WILLIAM CHILCOTT AND (2) MARY GAZZAM-LARWILL.

(*16*) *Joseph Hart ;* born January 12, 1783, at Chesterton, England. He came with his parents to this country, settling in Philadelphia. Afterwards he lived in Pittsburg, and later in Wooster, Ohio. After the death of his parents, he and his four brothers and two sisters resided in Wooster over half a century. He was a protege of General Jackson, whom he is said to have resembled mentally and physically. He was Receiver of the Land Office for many years. He died a very wealthy man, November 20, 1867. He married Nancy Quinby at Warren, Ohio, May 22, 1817. Of this marriage there was no issue. [Mrs. Nancy Quinby-Larwill was born May 9, 1793, and died at Wooster, July 23, 1893, aged 100 years, 2 months and 14 days.]

(*17*) *Julia Robinson;* born October 7, 1784, at Chesterton, England ; died February 17, 1861 ; married, in Fawcettstown, Ohio, May 13, 1813, John Fawcett [born January 13, 1784 ; died August 18, 1866]. The marriage was without issue.

(*18*) *William;* born December 30, 1786, at London, England ; died at Wooster, Ohio, February 14, 1861 ; married, at Georgetown, Pa., May 23, 1816, Susan Christmas. Mrs. William Christmas-Larwill was born January 10, 1795, and died at Washington, D. C., September 7, 1878. Of this marriage there was issue nine children :—

    (*79*) *Julia M.;* born March 30, 1817 ; died March 1, 1847.

    (*80*) *Mary G.;* born in 1819.

    (*81*) *John C.;* born February 20, 1821 ; a successful business man of Mansfield, Ohio.

    (*82*) *Levinia;* died in infancy.

    (*83*) *Elizabeth C.;* born in June, 1825.

    (*84*) *Lucretia;* died in infancy.

    (*85*) *William;* born November 8, 1829.

    (*86*) *Joseph H.;* born Dec. 25, 1833.

    (*87*) *Oscar;* born April 13, 1835; died July 4, 1859.

(*19*) *Mary ;* } born and died in 1788. Interred in
(*20*) *Benoni ;* } Bunhill Fields, London, England.

(*21*) *Mary B. ;* born November 5, 1790, at Deptford,
Kent County, England ; died April 26, 1873.

(*22*) *John ;* born September 27, 1792, at Deptford, Kent
County, England ; died March 19, 1875 ; married, at
Salem, Ohio, January 3, 1826, Ann Straughan [born in
Salem, Ohio, October 9, 1805 ; died June 7, 1886]. Of
this marriage there was issue seven children :—

    (*88*) *William G. ;* born August 25, 1827 ; died
February 11, 1830.

    (*89*) *Ann E. ;* born January 29, 1830.

    (*90*) *Martha H. ;* born April 13, 1831.

    (*91*) *Emma M. ;* born April 11, 1833.

    (*92*) *John S. ;* born April 12, 1835.

    (*93*) *Julia F. ;* born September 7, 1839 ; died
May 15, 1877.

    (*94*) Infant son, born and died December 31, 1843.

(*23*) *Ebenezer ;* born and died at Philadelphia, Pa., in
1795, aged 6 months, 9 days.

(*24*) *Jabez Brackenridge ;* born at Pittsburgh, Pa., December 2, 1799 ; died June 12, 1863 ; married, at Morgan-
town, Va., August 13, 1829, Amanda Jarrett. Mrs.
Amanda Jarrett-Larwill died at Wooster, Ohio, December
7, 1884, aged 76 years, 11 months, 7 days. Of this marriage was there issue nine children :—

    (*95*) *Joseph H.*
    (*96*) *Mary G.*
    (*97*) *Julia C.*
    (*98*) *William J.*
    (*99*) *John Fawcett.*
    (*100*) *Nancy Quinby.*

(*101*) *George M.*
(*102*) *Amanda J.*
(*103*) *Leroy J.*

THE CHILDREN OF DAVID AND (*6*) LYDIA GAZZAM-KIMPTON.

(*41*) *William Gazzam;* born in England; was a soldier in the War of 1812 ; died at Newark, Ohio.

(*42*) *David;* infant, buried at sea.

(*43*) *Joseph;* died at Philadelphia, Pa.

(*44*) *David;* died at Beulah, Pa., aged 18 months.

(*45*) *Lydia;* died November 7, 1824, at Wooster, Ohio.

(*46*) *Mary;* married George Blaney ; died 1836 or 1837.

(*47*) *Rebecca;* married Charles Blaney ; died at Gardiner, Ill., March 30, 1873.

(*48*) *Joshua;* died at Newark, Ohio, January 5, 1854, aged 47 years.

(*49*) *Mary Alice;* died at Columbus, Ohio, February 11, 1892, aged 84 years.

CHILDREN OF (*7*) JOSEPH AND ANN GOODCHEAP-GAZZAM.

(*50*) *Emma Goodcheap;* born July 25, 1796 ; died 1812 or 1813.

(*51*) *James;* born August 18, 1797 ; died April 19, 1798.

(*52*) *Ann;* born October 26, 1798 ; died May 11, 1811.

(*53*) *Joseph;* born August 7, 1800 ; died March 18, 1807.

(*54*) *Susannah;* born November 2, 1801.

(*55*) *Sarah;* born December 30, 1802 ; died October 15, 1825.

[From a picture in the possession of J. G. Butler, Atlanta, Ga.]

MRS. REBECCA GAZZAM-JONES.

(See page 6.)

(*56*) *Thomas Goodcheap;* born September 11, 1804 ; died April 19, 1805.

All lived and died in England.

CHILDREN OF EDWARD AND (*8*) REBECCA GAZZAM-JONES.

(*57*) *Rebecca Gazzam;* born October 23, 1795, at Philadelphia ; died September 9, 1878, at Indianapolis, Ind.

(*58*) *Edward Oldfield;* died September 30, 1838, at Matagorda, Tex.

(*59*) *Charles;* died August 19, 1839, at Pittsburg, Pa.

(*60*) *Emma Goodcheap;* missionary for 17 years, going to Shanghai, China, in 1845, with Bishop Boone, Episcopalian ; she died at Baltimore, Md., March 19, 1879. She never married.

(*61*) *Martha E.;* married, first, William W. Fry, of Mobile, Ala.; married, second, General Samuel Lewis, of Staunton, Va.; died at Staunton, July 27, 1870.

(*62*) *Anna Selina;* married George H. Fry, of Mobile, Ala., whom she survived. There were no children. She died at the home of her niece, Mrs. General Lew Wallace (wife of the distinguished author), at Indianapolis, Ind., September 25, 1891.

(*63*) *Mary Alice;* died August 8, 1813, in infancy, at Fawcettstown, Ohio.

THE CHILDREN OF WILLIAM AND (*9*) MARY ALICE GAZZAM-TAYLOR.

(*64*) *William Gazzam;* born at Philadelphia, May 6, 1795 ; died May 7, 1795.

(*65*) *Thomas Davis;* born at London, England, August 9, 1797, while his mother was there on a visit; died September 28, 1797.

(*66*) *Thomas William;* born at Philadelphia, December 14, 1798; died August 25, 1858, at Edina, Mo. He was twice married.

(*67*) *Benjamin Cook;* born at Philadelphia, February 24, 1801; died at Bergen, N. J., February 2, 1881. He married Anna Rome, of which union there was issue four children. (*See post, Nos. 155–158.*)

(*68*) *Othniel Hart;* born at Philadelphia, May 4, 1803; died September 5, 1869, at Camden, N. J. He was a physician of considerable reputation, practicing his profession at Camden for nearly thirty years. Previous to 1844 he was connected with several medical institutions at Philadelphia. In 1820 he entered the literary department of the University of Pennsylvania, and afterward took the medical course, graduating in 1826. Dr. Taylor's name appears as one of the incorporators of the Camden County Medical Society in 1846, he being its first vice president. In 1856 he became its president. He was the organizer of the Camden City Medical Society; also of the City Dispensary. In 1849, 1850 and 1851 he was the vice president of the New Jersey State Medical Society, and in 1852 was elected its president. He was a man of rare literary taste, and the author of many valuable works. For twenty-two years he was a warden of St. Paul's Protestant Episcopal Church. He married Evelina Constance Borrough, a descendant of the earliest settlers of English Quakers in West Jersey, namely, the Fenwicks, Adamses, Burroughs, Wallaces, Hollinsheads and Roberts, who came there over two hundred years ago. Of this marriage there was issue four children. (*See post, Nos. 159–162.*)

(*69*) *Mary Alice Hay ;* born at Philadelphia, November 20, 1804 ; died at Fairfield, Essex County, N. J.; married to the Rev. Joseph Wilson. Of this marriage there was issue five children. (*See post, Nos. 163–167*).

(*70*) *Sarah Fulton ;* born February 15, 1806; died March 4, 1806.

(*71*) *Martha Elizabeth ;* born October 25, 1809; married General Henry S. Genet. She now (1894) resides with her son at Bergen, N. J., being the only living grandchild of (*5*) William and Martha Gazzam. Her husband, Henry S. Genet, was the son of Count Edmond Charles Genet, first Minister of France to the United States ; projector of the Erie Canal and one of the founders of the Democratic party. Martha E. Genet was the mother of thirteen children. (*See post, Nos. 168–180*).

(*72*) *William Rivers ;* born at Philadelphia, October 22, 1810 ; died February 23, 1826.

(*73*) *Isaac Ebenezer ;* born April 25, 1812. At an early age he was admitted to practice as a physician, and in the pursuit of his profession attained considerable distinction. At the time of his death (in 1891) he was generally conceded to be one of the most skillful practitioners in New York City. He was chief physician of the Bellevue Medical Hospital. He was twice married, his first wife being Eliza May, youngest daughter of Stuart Mollan, of New York, and the second, Mrs. Emily Courtney, of New York. Of his marriage with Eliza May Mollan there was issue four children. (*See post, Nos. 181–184.*)

(*74*) *Joseph Gazzam ;* born February 12, 1815, at Philadelphia ; died at Greenbush, N. J., January 21, 1853. He was the father of seven children. (*See post, Nos. 185–191.*)

THE CHILDREN AND GRANDCHILDREN OF (67) BENJAMIN COOK AND ANNA ROME-TAYLOR.

(*155*) *Susannah ;* married a Mr. Harris.

(*156*) *Mary ;* married a Mr. Van Alen.   Of this marriage there was issue one son :—

    (*296*) *Henry ;* living in Hudson County, N. J.

(*157*) *William J. Romeyn ;* died in 1892.   He was a prominent minister, having had charge of the First Dutch Reformed Church, of New Brunswick, N. J., for many years.   At the time of his death he was identified with the American Bible Society.   He was the father of four sons:—

    (*297*) *Van Campen ;* architect.
    (*298*) *Southerland ;* minister.
    (*299*) *William ;* minister.
    (*300*) *Livingston ;* minister.

(*158*) *Isaac ;* a graduate of Rutger's College ; now one of the leading lawyers of Jersey City, with considerable practice as advisory master of the Court of Chancery.   He is married and has one daughter :—

    (*301*) *Bertha.*

THE CHILDREN OF (68) OTHNIEL HART AND EVELINA BURROUGH-TAYLOR.

(*159*) *Rivers ;* born at Philadelphia, January 5, 1833 ; died August 31, 1833.

(*160*) *Othniel Gazzam ;* born at Philadelphia, January 24, 1834 ; died at Camden, N. J., March 14, 1886.   He was a pharmacist of the Camden City Dispensary for thirty years.

(*161*) *Marmaduke Borrough ;* born at Philadelphia, August 17, 1835 ; died at Camden, N. J., January 15, 1890. He graduated from the Poughkeepsie, N. Y., Law School, and was admitted to the New Jersey Bar in 1856. He practiced law in Camden, being highly successful in his profession. In addition to being a counsellor, an attorney-at-law, solicitor in chancery and special master in chancery, he was United States commissioner for the Court of Claims, and held the office of clerk and solicitor for the Camden Board of Education for many years. He was secretary of the vestry of St. Paul's P. E. Church for years, and at the time of his death was the only warden of that church. He was counsellor for the Society of the Sons of St. George, Philadelphia. He had traveled over many of the countries of Europe, and lectured on the various cities for a number of the Masonic bodies. On September 3, 1861, he married Agnes Crain, daughter of Joseph and Rebecca Gibson Wills-Crain. Of this marriage there was issue three children. (*See post, Nos. 302–304.*)

(*162*) *Henry Genet;* born at Schodack, Rensalier County, N. J., July 6, 1837. He was a graduate of the Medical Department of the University of Pennsylvania. He entered, as assistant surgeon, the New Jersey Militia at the commencement of the Rebellion, and served throughout the war. He has been secretary of the Camden Medical Society for thirty-five years, and secretary of the Camden City Dispensary for thirty years. He has also been president of the Camden County Medical Society, of the Camden City Medical Society and of the New Jersey State Medical Society, and is now chief physician of the Cooper Hospital, of Camden. He married, October 23, 1879, Helen, daughter of Alexander and Hannah Cooper, of 305 Cooper street, Camden. Of this marriage there was issue three children. (*See post, Nos. 305–307.*)

THE CHILDREN OF JOSEPH AND (*69*) MARY A. H. TAYLOR-WILSON.

(*163*) *Benjamin.*
(*164*) *Theodore.*
(*165*) *Sarah.*
(*166*) *Louise.*
(*167*) *Jane.*

THE CHILDREN OF HENRY JAMES AND (*71*) MARTHA ELIZABETH TAYLOR-GENET.

(*168*) *Edmond Charles ;* deceased.
(*169*) *William Rivers ;* deceased.
(*170*) *Martha Elizabeth ;* single.
(*171*) *Henry James ;* deceased.
(*172*) *Mary Alice ;* deceased.
(*173*) *Cornelia Clinton* (Mrs. Lockhart Mackie).
(*174*) *George Clinton ;* single.
(*175*) *Louise Henrietta ;* single.
(*176*) *Henry Alexander ;* married.
(*177*) *Eugenie Spencer* (Mrs. E. Bloodgood).
(*178*) *Louis Franklin Facio ;* married.
(*179*) *Josephine Adele ;* single.
(*180*) *Julie Othnelia ;* deceased.

THE CHILDREN OF (*73*) ISAAC EBENEZER AND ELIZA MAY MOLLAN-TAYLOR.

(*181*) *Stuart ;* married Gertrude Judge, of Georgia.
(*182*) *Emily ;* married to Pierre Lorillard, of New York.

(*183*) *Ann Jane ;* married to Hilliard Meany Judge (brother of Mrs. Gertrude Judge-Taylor).

(*184*) *Louise ;* unmarried.

The above are all living.

THE CHILDREN OF (*74*) JOSEPH GAZZAM TAYLOR.

(*185*) *Rivers.*
(*186*) *Elizabeth.*
(*187*) *Clinton.*
(*188*) *William.*
(*189*) *Joseph.*
(*190*) *Theodore.*
(*191*) *Southerland.*

THE CHILDREN OF (*161*) MARMADUKE BURROUGH AND AGNES CRAIN-TAYLOR.

(*302*) *Clarence Wills ;* born at Camden, N. J., July 11, 1862. He is a graduate of the Protestant Episcopal College, class of '80 ; and of the University of Pennsylvania, College Department, class of '84. He is now (1894) engaged in the real estate business at Camden, having entered it upon his graduation. He is a director of the Penn Electric Light Company, of the American Color Printing Company, and of the Weil Gas Enriching Company, besides being the owner of several large tracts of woodland and meadow in South Jersey ; also of the Taylor Building, in Camden. He is a member of the Pennsylvania Society of the Cincinnati, the New Jersey Sons of the Revolution (from eight ancestors), and of the Society of the War of 1812, of Pennsylvania ; a member of St. Paul's P. E. Church, Camden; of the Camden City Board of Trade, and Camden Republican Club.

(*303*) *Evelina Constance ;* born December 5, 1865 ; died February 3, 1870.

(*304*) *Annie ;* born September 3, 1871. She is a member of the New Jersey Society of the Colonial Dames (from ten ancestors). She was married November 2, 1893, to Rev. Robert Atkinson Mays, Rector of Holy Trinity Memorial P. E. Church, Twenty-second and Pine streets, Philadelphia. Mr. Mays is a graduate of Princeton, class of '78 ; of Columbia Law School, class of '80 ; and the University of Virginia Theological Seminary, class of '84.

THE CHILDREN OF (*162*) HENRY GENET AND HANNAH COOPER-TAYLOR.

(*305*) *Henry Genet ;* born July 19, 1883.

(*306*) *Richard Cooper ;* born September 29, 1884.

(*307*) *Helen Elizabeth ;* born February 27, 1887 ; died March, 1889.

All born at Camden, N. J.

(5) WILLIAM GAZZAM.

William Gazzam, the eldest son of William and Martha Gazzam, was educated at the University of Cambridge, and became an eminent journalist in England during the latter half of the eighteenth century. He was remembered there as a very quiet man, but one who possessed liberal ideas and high ideals, which he expressed with great vigor and trenchant pen. Although his writings attracted wide attention in England, he never cared to take any credit to himself for public good attained thereby, preferring to remain the unknown power behind the throne. He published a newspaper at Cambridge, and in it said many things that were not altogether to the liking of the King. Being an ardent lover of freedom, he naturally sympathized with the people of America, asserting the eminent justice of their wished-for autonomy. In this opinion, it will be remembered, the King failed to concur. Therefore, the liberal writings of Mr. Gazzam, probably in much exaggerated recital, coming often to official attention, it naturally followed that steps were finally taken to suppress the utterances of the intrepid journalist of freedom. Purposing his arrest, it is not unlikely the Crown would have welcomed his death, since a patriot and fast friend of Mr. Gazzam's, Edward Despard,* was executed about this time for similar utterances.

Warned of his impending danger, Mr. Gazzam made a hasty flight from the country. America was naturally his prospective bourne, though he first went to Paris, where he remained a short time, being in that city at the time of the

*See Biographical Sketch of (31) Edward Despard Gazzam; post.

execution of Louis XVI (January 21, 1793). Shortly afterward he returned to England, whence he embarked with
his family for the land of the free.

The following letter, written by the celebrated author of
" Rippon's Hymns," will convey some idea of Mr. Gazzam's
precipitate departure from England, as well as of the esteem
in which he was held by his neighbors :—

LONDON, February 6, 1793.

To the Rev. Dr. Rogers, the Rev. Dr. Eusticks, of Philadelphia ; the
Rev. Dr. Foster, of New York ; the Rev. Dr. Edwards, of New Haven,
Conn.; the Rev. Dr. Lillman, of Boston ; the Rev. Dr. Hood, of Lex-
ington, or to any other of my American correspondents to whom this
may come :—

This is to certify that Mr. William Gazzam, the bearer of these lines,
is an honorable member of the Congregational Church at Cambridge, under the pastoral care of Rev. Mr. Grier. He has been driven from his
own country only for speaking in behalf of the rights of mankind—per-
haps incautiously. So hasty was his removal that his much-loved pastor
had no opportunity to give him testimonials. He is united with one of
our Baptist families, and with others of our friends, whose names would
gladly be united in recommending him and his attention to our foreign
friends, with the name of their obliged and affectionate brother and
servant,   JOHN RIPPON.

In due course of time the fugitive reached Philadelphia,
Pa., where, on July 20, 1793, he affirmed allegiance to the
Commonwealth of Pennsylvania, and soon became well and
favorably known as a public-spirited citizen. In this country his great love for freedom and his constant advocacy of
it took a new direction, and he became an active member
of the old " Philadelphia Society for the Abolition of
Slavery and the Amelioration of the Condition of the
Colored People." This was a Quaker Society, for, though
not a Friend, he observed many of their customs, among
them being the constant refusal to take an oath, always
" affirming " when occasion required. During his resi-

dence at Philadelphia he became a member of the Second Presbyterian Church.

Shortly after his arrival in the Quaker City Mr. Gazzam engaged in mercantile business at No. 20 North Front Street. In those days importing merchants usually owned the ships they freighted, it requiring a large amount of capital to embark in this line of business, and Joseph Hart, a kinsman, who was a bachelor of considerable means, furnishing the necessary funds for Mr. Gazzam, the enterprise started and flourished.

In 1796 the bookkeeper of the house, Mr. William Taylor, was taken into partnership, the firm being designated as Gazzam & Taylor, and the next year Mr. Edward Jones, a clerk, was admitted, the firm becoming Gazzam, Taylor & Jones. At the same time the place of business was removed to No. 36 North Second Street. Mr. Taylor withdrew in 1800 or 1801, and the firm became Gazzam & Jones, a partnership which was dissolved a year later. Mr. Hart, brother of Martha Gazzam, wife of (*1*) William Gazzam, the European agent of the American house, purchased and shipped the goods sold by it ; and during the troubles with France one of the firm's vessels, a brig laden with teas, was seized by French privateers, the heavy loss sustained falling, it seems, entirely upon Mr. Gazzam, a loss for which neither he nor his heirs have ever received indemnity.

In 1802 Mr. Gazzam moved to Pittsburg, Pa., where he passed the remainder of his life. On March 31, 1808, he was appointed first Collector of the Port of Pittsburg by President Jefferson, being recommended for the place by James Madison, then Secretary of State.* He was also ap-

---

*His commission as Collector and his certificates of marriage and membership in the Philadelphia Society are in the possession of (*108*) J. B. Gazzam, of St. Louis.

pointed magistrate by Governor Snyder, at that time an office of dignity and importance.

He married twice, his first wife being Elizabeth Scaiffe, of Cambridge, England, who, with their three children, accompanied Mr. Gazzam to America. Mrs. Elizabeth Gazzam died at Philadelphia, Pa., during the first year of her residence in this country. Six months after her decease, May 19, 1794, Mr. Gazzam married Ann Parker, of. Philadelphia.

(*5*) William Gazzam died in Pittsburg, November 16, 1811, aged forty-eight years. His second wife, Ann Parker, who was born in September, 1776, died March 7, 1843, at Allegheny, Pa. They are buried in Allegheny Cemetery, Lot No. 28, Section 19.

THE CHILDREN OF (*5*) WILLIAM GAZZAM.

William Gazzam was the father of sixteen children, those by his first wife, Elizabeth Scaiffe-Gazzam, being :—

(*25*) *William ;* served in the War of 1812, from November 9, 1813, to November 9, 1814, having enlisted as a private in Captain Samuel Morris' company of Sea Fencibles, from Philadelphia. He died in Texas, leaving a family of children, one of whom was a Confederate prisoner of war.

(*26*) *Anna ;* born May 11, 1790 ; married Samuel Bucknall, of Philadelphia, December 14, 1814 ; died November 14, 1873. Of this marriage there was issue four children. (*See post, Nos. 104–107.*)

(*27*) *Elizabeth ;* married her cousin, William Gazzam Kimpton ; died at Newark, Ohio.

MRS. ANN PARKER GAZZAM.

(See page 33.)

Those by his second wife, Ann Parker-Gazzam, were :—

(*28*) *Sarah ;* born May 10, 1796 ; died August 16, 1855.

(*29*) *Joseph Parker ;* born at Philadelphia, Pa., February 1, 1797 ; died at Pittsburg, Pa., May 29, 1863; a practicing physician.   He married, at Brownsville, Pa., December 28, 1824, Harriet Breading, daughter of Judge Nathaniel and Mary Ewing Breading, of Fayette County, Pa., who was born May 11, 1803, and died at Pittsburg, August 27, 1838.   Both are buried in Allegheny Cemetery.   Of this marriage there was issue two children.   (*See post*, *108–109*.)

(*30*) *Charles Wood ;* born March 7, 1798 ; died at Mobile, Ala., October 13, 1882.   Born at Philadelphia, he went with his father to Pittsburg.   He married, at Pittsburg, Clementina Lea, a member of the Lea family, of the old Philadelphia publishing house of Carey, Lea & Carey. He resided for many years at Cincinnati, Ohio, where he amassed a large fortune, passing the last years of a long and useful life in the city (Mobile) in which he died.   He was the founder of many business enterprises, among them being the Mobile Foundry Company, the first iron manufacturing company in the South ; and was the president of the First National Bank of Mobile from its establishment until the time of his death ; of the Mobile Savings Bank, and of the Fulton Cotton Factory.   He was the patron of Hiram Powers, having furnished the great sculptor with the money necessary to pursue his studies and travels. Mrs. Clementina Lea-Gazzam died September 21, 1886. There was issue of this marriage eleven children.   (*See post, Nos. 110–120.*)

(*31*) *Catharine Selina ;* born April 26, 1799 ; died at Boston, Mass., January 28, 1882 ; married at Pittsburg, May 1, 1821, by Rev. Joseph McElroy, to John Bartlett

24

Butler, the son of John Butler, of the State of New York.
The latter, having left his farm and entered the Continental
Army, served three years during the War of the Revolution. [John Bartlett Butler was born in Columbia County,
N. Y., May 6, 1793, having had four brothers and four sisters, who settled in various parts of New York and Con-
necticut. At 19 years of age he entered a printing office
in New York City. In the War of 1812 he served for six
months in the defenses of Baltimore, and shortly afterwards
removed to Ravenna, Ohio, where he established a newspaper. After a few years he settled at Pittsburg, being
editor and proprietor of the Pittsburg *Statesman*. After
an editorial career of twenty-seven years he sold his paper,
having been appointed president of the Pennsylvania Canal
Commission, which position he resigned at the outbreak of
the Mexican War to accept an appointment as major on
the staff of General Taylor. At the close of the war he
was commissioned paymaster and military storekeeper in
the Regular Army, with the rank of captain, and stationed
at the Allegheny Arsenal, Pittsburg. He retired from the
army at the close of the War of the Rebellion, in 1866, and
died at Cincinnati, Ohio, December 7, 1870.] Of the marriage of John Bartlett Butler and Catharine Gazzam-Butler
there was issue ten children. (*See post, Nos. 121–130.*)

(*32*) *Louisa Parker;* born in 1800; died in 1806. She
was accidentally burned to death.

(*33*) *Audley Hart;* born in 1801; died at Baltimore,
Md., April 7, 1893; married, at Paris, France, in August,
1844, Marguerite de Loche. Of this marriage there was
issue one daughter. (*See post, No. 131.*)

(*34*) *Edward Despard;* born at Pittsburg in 1803; died
at Philadelphia, February 19, 1878.*

---

*See biographical sketch; post.

25

(*35*) *Mary Alice;* born at Pittsburg, November 24, 1804 ; died at Muscatine, Iowa, January 9, 1892 ; married to Sage O. Butler, June 10, 1833. Of this marriage there was issue six children. (*See post, Nos. 135–140.*)

(*36*) *Ebenezer;* born at Pittsburg in 1806 ; died at Allegheny City, August 13, 1881. In 1834 married Elizabeth Ann Stevenson [who was born January 18, 1818, and died April 6, 1891]. Of this marriage there was issue fourteen children. (*See post, Nos. 141–154.*)

(*37*) (*38*) (*39*) (*40*) Children who died in infancy.

THE CHILDREN OF SAMUEL AND (*26*) ANNA GAZZAM-BUCKNALL.

(*104*) *Joanna Rooker;* born December 9, 1815. Living (1894).

(*105*) *Ebenezer Gazzam;* born November 29, 1819. Living, unmarried (1894).

(*106*) *Samuel Rooker;* born July 9, 1817 ; died February 22, 1888 ; married, March, 1848, Lydia S. Eastlack. Of this marriage there was issue two sons. (*See post, Nos. 192–193.*)

(*107*) *Martha Elizabeth;* born November 19, 1821; died, unmarried, June 15, 1880.

THE CHILDREN AND GRANDCHILDREN OF (*106*) SAMUEL ROOKER AND LYDIA EASTLACK-BUCKNALL.

(*192*) *Simeon Eastlack;* born May 16, 1850 ; married, August 5, 1873, Marion Augusta Cochran. Of this marriage there was issue five children :—

(*308*) *Nellie Lydia ;* born June 25, 1874.
(*309*) *Samuel Kazlett ;* born January 6, 1876.
(*310*) *Martha Elizabeth ;* born Dec. 11, 1877.
(*311*) *Marion Augusta ;* born April 1, 1878.
(*312*) *Anna Maria ;* born February 24, 1880.

(*193*) **Samuel ;* born September 13, 1852 ; married, November 22, 1882, Rebekah Russell.   Of this marriage there was issue three children :—

(*313*) *George Gordon ;* born September 16, 1883 ; died April 9, 1891.
(*314*) *Mary Russell ;* born August 14, 1885.
(*315*) *Lydia Eastlack ;* born April 20, 1887.

THE CHILDREN OF (*29*) JOSEPH PARKER AND HARRIET
BREADING-GAZZAM.

(*108*) *James Breading ;* born at Pittsburg, May 4, 1833. Removed in 1853 to St. Louis, Mo., where he still lives. Married, October 27, 1859, Louisa Morris, daughter of John Logan and Louisa Morris-Blaine, of Frankford, Ky.   Mrs. James Breading-Gazzam was born May 2, 1836.   Of this marriage there was issue one child :—

(*194*) *Joseph Parker ;* born at St. Louis, Mo., January 26, 1861.

(*109*) *Harriet Breading ;* born June 10, 1836 ; died, unmarried, in April, 1854.   Buried in Allegheny Cemetery, Allegheny City, Pa.

---

*The sons of (*106*) Samuel R. Bucknall (Simeon E. and Samuel) spell their names with the original "e" instead of "a," which change was made by the grandfather of S. R. B. in his declining years.

DR. JOSEPH P. GAZZAM

(See page 25.)

THE CHILDREN OF (*30*) CHARLES WOOD AND CLEMENTINA GAZZAM.

(*110*) *Catharine Selina;* born at Cincinnati, O., September 1, 1828 ; married, February 21, 1850, to Judge John A. Hitchcock, whom she survived. Now living at Spring Hill, near Mobile, Ala. No issue.

(*111*) *Audley Hart;* born at Cincinnati, August 7, 1830; died in infancy.

(*112*) *George Gano;* born October 22, 1831 ; died in the Confederate Army, September 1, 1864. Married, April 25, 1860, Lucy A. Schuyler, of Mobile, Ala. Of this marriage there was issue one daughter :—

> (*195*) *Kate Lea;* married at Mobile, Ala., to H. G. Donald, of England. Of this marriage there was issue two sons and several daughters.

(*113*) } Twin sons, born October 24, 1833 ; died in in-
(*114*) } fancy.

(*115*) *Charles Wood;* born at Cincinnati, Ohio, August 29, 1834; moved with his mother to Mobile, Ala., in 1839, where he was employed in his father's banks. He served through the War of the Rebellion in Bragg's army. He married, August 28, 1860, Mary G. Thomas, at Mobile. Of this marriage there was issue six children. (*See post, Nos. 196–201*).

(*116*) *Clement Lea;* born at Cincinnati, January 3, 1837; died at Mobile, January 26, 1851.

(*117*) *William Parker;* born at Cincinnati, April 29, 1839 ; went to Mobile when an infant ; was educated in Virginia and entered business in New Orleans, La. He served in General Lee's Confederate Army, and married, December 5, 1882, Helen Maermurdo. Of this marriage there is no issue (1894).

(*118*) *Henry McClyment;* born at Mobile, September 13, 1841. Served in General Hood's Confederate army. Died at Mobile, August 7, 1877. Married, in Texas, Sarah A. Holland. Of this marriage there was issue one child:—

(*202*) *Selina.*

(*119*) *Claudius Douglas;* born February 1, 1844 ; died September 22, 1877.

(*120*) *John Lea ;* born November 8, 1846 ; died May 29, 1849.

———

THE CHILDREN AND GRANDCHILDREN OF (*115*) CHARLES WOOD AND MARY G. THOMAS-GAZZAM.

(*196*) *Warren Lea ;* born June 8, 1863 ; married at Seattle, Washington, where he resided for a number of years. He is now living at Portland, Oregon. He is the father of two children :—

(*316*) *Lea.*
(*317*)

(*197*) *George Goodwin;* born February 24, 1866 ; died in 1869.

(*198*) *Mary ;* born October 16, 1867 ; married to Archibald J. Fisken, of Seattle. Of this marriage there is issue (1894) two sons :—

(*318*) *Keith Gazzam.*
(*319*) *Archibald Donald;* born April 14, 1894.

(*199*) *Clement ;* born January 19, 1869 ; a missionary at Colon, Columbia, Central America.

(*200*) *Lucy ;* born October 8, 1872.

(*201*) *Emily Lea ;* born March 30, 1876.

THE CHILDREN AND GRANDCHILDREN OF JOHN BARTLETT
AND (*31*) CATHARINE SELINA GAZZAM-BUTLER.

(*121*) *Charles Junius;* born at Pittsburg, March 6,
1822 ; married Margaret E. Lansing, in 1846.   Of this marriage there was issue five children :—

> (*203*) *Margaret E. Lansing ;* died.
> (*204*) *Gertrude Letitia ;* married.
> (*205*) *Robert Lansing ;* married.
> (*206*) *George Jackson.*
> (*207*) *Fannie Elizabeth ;* died.

(*122*) *Joseph Curran;* born December 23, 1823 ; died
June 13, 1873.   Married Alice Lafferty.   Of this marriage
there was issue nine children :—

> (*208*) *Kate Una ;* died March 1, 1851.
> (*209*) *John Bryant;* died September 15, 1865.
> (*210*) *Pierce Ormond.*
> (*211*) *Kenneth Lafferty;* married.
> (*212*) *Alice.*
> (*213*) *Florence.*
> (*214*) *Honoria.*
> (*215*) *Joseph.*
> (*216*) *Mary.*

(*123*) *Frances Ann ;* born September 28, 1825 ; married,
May 21, 1846, to Dr. Albert G. Walter [born at Augesburg,
Prussia, June 21, 1811 ; died at Pittsburg, Pa., October 14,
1876].   Of this marriage there was issue four children.
(*See post, Nos. 217–220*).

(*124*) *Harriet Elizabeth;* born September 30, 1827 ;
married to Samuel J. R. McMillan (late United States Senator), October 31, 1850, at the Allegheny Arsenal, Pitts-

burg, Pa. Of this marriage there was issue nine children. (*See post, Nos. 221–229*).

(*125*) *Sarah Prudence ;* born December 23, 1829 : died January 6, 1852. Married to Austin Loomis at Pittsburg, in 1851. Of this marriage there was issue one child :—

> (*230*) *Austin Butler ;* born in 1851; died in 1880.

(*126*) *Kate Aurelia ;* born March 9, 1832 ; died April 30, 1858.

(*127*) *Richard Audley ;* born December 29, 1834 ; married Lydia Davis. Of this marriage there was issue four children. (*See post, Nos. 231–234*).

(*128*) *Caroline Sydney ;* born October 31, 1838 ; married to Dr. David Day, September 29, 1858, at Pittsburg, Pa. Of this marriage there was issue five children :—

> (*235*) *Gordon Butler ;* died.
> (*236*) *David Henry ;* married.
> (*237*) *Charles Butler.*
> (*238*) *Alice.*
> (*239*) *Lillian Warnick.*

(*129*) *John Gazzam ;* born at Pittsburg, Pa., January 23, 1842. Appointed cadet at the United States Military Academy, West Point, in 1859. Graduated in 1863. Was appointed second lieutenant in Battery M, 4th U. S. Artillery, joining the Union Army in the field. He was promoted for gallant conduct in the battle of Chickamauga, and examined and promoted to the ordnance corps of the army in 1864. After the close of the war he served as contractor and inspector of ordnance at Boston, West Point, Reading, Philadelphia and Pittsburg foundries, and later served at various arsenals, and at the National Armory, and again as assistant constructor of ordnance in New York from 1873 to 1876. In command of the St. Louis powder depot from 1887 to 1890, and from the latter date to the present time (1894) in command of the arsenal at Augusta, Ga. Married at Philadelphia, Pa., January 25, 1866, Eliza (called Lillie) M. Warnick. Of this marriage there was issue six children :—

(*240*) *Mary Warnick.*
(*241*) *Lawrence Parker.*
(*242*) *Harriet McMillan.*
(*243*) *Rodman.*
(*244*) *Rollins.*
(*245*) *Lillie.*

(*130*) *Alice Olmstead;* born June 22, 1845; married to George T. Tilden, at Cincinnati, Ohio, October 5, 1871. Of this marriage there was issue four children :—

(*246*) *Laura May;* died January 12, 1876.
(*247*) *Charles Joseph.*
(*248*) *Alice Foster.*
(*249*) *Edith Selina.*

All the children of John Bartlett and (*31*) Catharine Selina Gazzam-Butler were born at Pittsburg, Pa.

———

THE CHILDREN AND GRANDCHILDREN OF DR. ALBERT G. AND (*123*) FRANCES ANN BUTLER-WALTER.

(*217*) *Joseph Gazzam;* born July 1, 1847; married Mary E. Dean, February 27, 1877. Of this marriage there was issue three children :—

(*320*) *Helen;* born August 8, 1878.
(*321*) *Alexander Dean;* born June 11, 1882.
(*322*) *Albert Gustav;* born July 27, 1886.

(*218*) *Selina Louisa ;* born April 10, 1850 ; died March 18, 1854.

(*219*) *Sarah Loomis ;* born December 3, 1852 ; died March 18, 1854.

(*220*) *Augusta Hammer ;* born January 3, 1855 ; married, February 24, 1881, to Dr. William Wallace, who died August 25, 1883. Of this marriage there was issue two children :—

> (*323*) *Selina Gazzam ;* born August 14, 1882 ; died October 31, 1882.
>
> (*324*) *Albert Walter ;* born October 31, 1883.

THE CHILDREN AND GRANDCHILDREN OF SAMUEL J. R. AND (*124*) HARRIET ELIZABETH BUTLER-MCMILLAN.

(*221*) *Catharine Gazzam ;* married, April 28, 1875, to James B. Beals, whom she survives (1894). Of this marriage there was issue two sons :—

> (*325*) *Walter Burgess.*
> (*326*) *James Burrie.*

(*222*) *John Butler ;* died.

(*223*) *Austin Loomis ;* died.

(*224*) *Anna Walter ;* married, September 1, 1880, to Frank P. Shepard, of St. Paul, Minn. Of this marriage there was issue three children :—

> (*327*) *David Chauncey.*
> (*328*) *Samuel McMillan.*
> (*329*) *Roger Bulkley.*

(*225*) *Joseph Butler.*
(*226*) *Jessie Garmily.*

SAMUEL J. R. McMILLAN.

(See page 29.)

(*227*) *Albert Walter.*
(*228*) *Thomas Erskine;* died, aged 4 years and 4 months.
(*229*) *Samuel Benedick.*

THE CHILDREN AND GRANDCHILDEN OF (*127*) RICHARD
AUDLEY AND LYDIA DAVIS-BUTLER.

(*231*) *Lina Louise;* married to Charles T. Moore. Of
this marriage there was issue two children :—

   (*330*) *Grace.*
   (*331*) *Alice.*

(*232*) *Ormond;* died July 28, 1875.
(*233*) *Caroline Day.*
(*234*) *Audley Richard.*

THE DAUGHTER AND GRANDCHILDREN OF (*33*) AUDLEY
HART AND MARGUERITE DE LOCHE-GAZZAM.

(*131*) *Marguerite;* born September 4, 1845 ; married, at
Baltimore, Md., October 19, 1865, to Louis Stow. Of this
marriage there was issue two children :

   (*250*) *Audley Hart;* born January 21, 1867.
   (*251*) *Edith;* born April 27, 1869 ; married, December 3, 1890, to Alexander Percy White, of
   Philadelphia.

THE CHILDREN AND GRANDCHILDREN OF SAGE O. AND
(*35*) MARY ALICE GAZZAM-BUTLER.

(*135*) *Clementina G.;* died in infancy.

(*136*) *Frederick Tomlin;* died in infancy.

(*137*) *Elizabeth O.;* born March 16, 1842.

(*138*) *Audley G.;* born at Cincinnati, Ohio, December 11, 1843 ; married Adela Vesey at Moliere, Ill., December 24, 1868. Of this marriage there was issue eight children, all born at Muscatine, Iowa.:—

> (*267*) *Ellis P.;* born December 5, 1869.
> (*268*) *Adela V. (Daisy);* born March 25, 1872.
> (*269*) *George O.;* born December 8, 1873.
> (*270*) *Alice (Pearl);* born November 7, 1876.
> (*271*) *Lawrence L.;* born January 10, 1878.
> (*272*) *Elizabeth L.;* born August 11, 1879.
> (*273*) *Frederick Daut;* born October 10, 1883.
> (*274*) *Edith O.;* born April 1, 1886.

(*139*) *W. Norman;* born at St. Louis, Mo., April 5, 1847.

(*140*) *Lawrence;* born at St. Louis, Mo., March, 1851 ; died at Muscatine, Iowa, January 24, 1878.

CHILDREN OF (*36*) EBENEZER AND ELIZABETH ANN STEVENSON-GAZZAM.

(*141*) *Ann Elizabeth;* died in childhood.

(*142*) *Letitia Jackson;* died in 1875; married Ross A. Workman. Of this marriage there was issue eight children. (*See post, Nos. 275–282*).

(*143*) *William Thomas;* married Elizabeth Shell; no children.

(*144*) *Charles Edward.*

(*145*) *Antoinette;* died in childhood.

(*146*) *George J.;* married Ann Russell. Of this marriage there was issue four children. (*See post, Nos. 283–286*).

(*147*) *John Butler;* married Susan Cherry. Of this marriage there was issue one child :—

    (*287*) *Florence.*

(*148*) *Joseph;* died in childhood.

(*149*) *Harriet Elizabeth.*

(*150*) *Sarah Selina.*

(*151*) *Henry Parker;* married Jane Harris. Of this marriage there was issue five children. (*See post, Nos. 288–292*).

(*152*) *Franklin Breading;* married Catharine Kanan. Of this marriage there was issue three children. (*See post, Nos. 293–295*).

(*153*) *Mary Butler;* died in childhood.

(*154*) *Clara Levinia.*

THE CHILDREN AND GRANDCHILDREN OF ROSS A. AND (*142*) LETITIA GAZZAM-WORKMAN.

(*275*) *Elizabeth;* married to J. V. Newman. Of this marriage there was issue three children :—

    (*345*) *Charles F.*
    (*346*) *John R.*
    (*347*) *Jessie.*

(*276*) *John Q.;* married Dora Scott. Of this marriage there was issue four children :—

    (*348*) *Myrtle.*
    (*349*) *Gertrude.*

(*350*) *Selina.*
(*351*) *Arden.*

(*277*) *Amanda ;* unmarried.

(*278*) *Ross A. ;* married Nannie Sutton. Of this marriage there was issue three children :—

(*352*) *Goldie.*
(*353*) *Earl Gazzam.*
(*354*) *Pearl.*

(*279*) *Selina B.;* married to B. D. Cobbs. Of this marriage there was issue four children :

(*355*) *Mary.*
(*356*) *Chester.*
(*357*) *Luther.*
(*358*)

(*280*) *Harriet.*
(*281*) *Henrietta.*
(*282*) *Frank.*

THE CHILDREN OF (*146*) GEORGE J. AND ANNIE RUSSELL-GAZZAM.

(*283*) *Elizabeth A.*
(*284*) *Annie A.*
(*285*) *May ;* died.
(*286*) *Letitia.*

THE CHILDREN OF (*151*) HENRY PARKER AND JANE HARRIS-GAZZAM.

(*288*) *Audley ;* died.

(*289*) *Clara.*
(*290*) *Elizabeth.*
(*291*) *Henry Parker.*
(*292*) *John Harris.*

————

THE CHILDREN OF (*152*) FRANK B. AND CATHARINE KANAN-
GAZZAM.

(*293*) *Nellie B.*
(*294*) *Mary.*
(*295*) *Frank.*

(34) EDWARD DESPARD GAZZAM.

The fourth son of (5) William and Ann Gazzam, who was born at Pittsburg in 1803, was, for a month or two, called Albert Gallatin, in honor of the great philanthropist, statesman and author of that name. But the boy's father met, it seems, with a grievous disappointment in one of his favorite great men, and so one day, after pondering the matter over, he said :—

"Wife, Albert Gallatin is not dead yet ; he may change before he leaves this world. Suppose we call this boy Edward Despard ?"*

So the boy was named for the Irish patriot.

He was given a liberal education. When he became nearly of age he commenced the study of law under the preceptorship of the Hon. Richard Biddle, whose law partner he afterward became. He was admitted to the Bar of Allegheny County in 1826. After practicing for two years he was compelled to abandon this profession on account of ill-health. Later he commenced the study of medicine, and in due time graduated from the University of Pennsylvania.

Dr. Gazzam was a man of the rarest intellectual attainments, and always took a keen interest in the development of the Republic, having inherited all his father's great love of freedom. He thus naturally drifted into Pennsylvania politics, in which he became an important factor, and a nomination for Congress was conferred upon him early in his political career. In the contest that followed he was defeated by a single vote. Reared in the Democratic faith, like many of the same school he was bitterly opposed to

---

*See page 19.

DR. EDWARD D. GAZZAM.

(See page 38).

the extension of slavery. On this account he severed his connection with Democracy, and in 1848, together with Salmon P. Chase (afterward Chief Justice of the United States) and others, assisted in founding the Free Soil Party in the memorable Buffalo Convention. In the same year he became the Free Soil candidate for Governor of Pennsylvania, his opponents being William F. Johnson, Whig (who was elected), and Morris Longstreth, Democrat.

In 1855 Dr. Gazzam was the Free Soil candidate for State Senator from Pittsburg. He was defeated in this contest, but the next year he was again put forward, this time as the candidate of the Union Republican Party. Being elected, by about one thousand majority over the combined votes of his two opponents, he thus became the first Republican Senator from Allegheny County. In 1857 he was prominently mentioned as Republican candidate for Governor, and had a large number of counties instructed for him, but withdrew from the contest before the Convention met.

Dr. Gazzam was also Postmaster at Pittsburg at one time. When Lafayette visited this country, in 1824, Dr. Gazzam was selected to make the welcoming speech in behalf of the people of Western Pennsylvania, at Pittsburg. In the performance of this duty he acquired considerable distinction on account of his youth and the excellence of his address.

Upon the breaking out of the Civil War Dr. Gazzam and Dr. McCook, of Pittsburg, were the first persons who took steps toward preventing Secretary of War Floyd from removing the guns, ammunition and other property of the United States from the Allegheny Arsenal. They telegraphed, on behalf of the Committee of Safety, to Washington regarding the removal, and in response received the following :—

ORDNANCE OFFICE, WASHINGTON, D. C., }
May 3, 1861. }

E. D. GAZZAM, Chairman, Pittsburg, Pa.:

Sir :—Your telegram of May 1 to the Secretary of War about powder now held by the Committee is received and sent to this office. If any of the powder is needed by the commanding officer of Allegheny Arsenal, and is, in his judgment, of suitable quality for the United States service, it may be delivered to him. The Committee must use their discretion about the residue, throwing every proper guard around the disposition to be made of it.

Respectfully, Your Obedient Servant,

JAMES W. RIPLEY, Lt.-Col. U. S. A.

The powder referred to was seized by the Committee of Safety when about to be shipped to a point within the jurisdiction of the Southern States, from which the importance of the step taken can be readily discerned.

On March 24, 1835, Dr. Gazzam married Elizabeth Antoinette deBeelen.* Three children were born to them :—

(*132*) *Audley William.*†

(*133*) *Emma Louise.*†

(*134*) *Joseph Murphy.*†

In 1867 Dr. Gazzam retired from active life and removed to Philadelphia, where he died January 19, 1878, and was buried in Allegheny Cemetery, where the remains of his wife also repose.

*See deBeelen family; post.   †See biographical sketches; post.

(*132*) AUDLEY WILLIAM GAZZAM.

Audley William, the eldest son of (*31*) Edward Despard Gazzam and Elizabeth Antoinette, his wife, was born in the city of Pittsburg, May 8, 1836. Receiving an excellent education, he began the study of law at a comparatively early age, and in due time was admitted to the Allegheny County Bar.

At the breaking out of the War of the Rebellion he was president of the Firemen's Association of Pittsburg, from which body he organized a company of volunteers, known as the " Fire Zouaves," of which he became captain. This company was placed under command of Generals Oakes and Casey, in Virginia, and captured the first cannon taken during the war, in an engagement on the Kanawha, about sixty miles from Wheeling, W. Va. Subsequently elected major of the One-Hundred-and-Third Regiment, Pennsylvania Volunteers, he commanded this regiment in the many actions in which it participated, always behaving gallantly, and at the battle of Fair Oaks was severely wounded in the head by a piece of shell. Later on he served in the United States Veteran Reserve Corps until July, 1865, when he resigned from the army and removed to Utica, N. Y.

Mr. Gazzam was well known in Pittsburg, New York, and Philadelphia as a lawyer of ability, making a specialty of bankruptcy cases. This branch of the law is indebted to him for several important works, among them being " Gazzam on Bankruptcy," and a " Digest of American and English Decisions in Bankruptcy."

Audley William Gazzam died at his home in the city of Philadelphia, on Saturday, May 10, 1884, after an illness of but a few hours. At the time of his death he was attor-

ney for the National Cremation Society, of which method
of disposal of the dead he was a strong advocate, and he
was the first member of that society to be cremated, incin-
eration taking place at the Le Moyne Crematory, at Washington, Pa., then the only crematory in the country.

Mr. Gazzam was married twice ; the first time at Pitts-
burg, Pa., to Mary Elizabeth Van Deusen, daughter of Rev.
Edwin M. Van Deusen, formerly rector of St. Peter's P. E.
Church, Pittsburg, and of Grace Church, Utica, N. Y.

Mrs. Mary Gazzam died in Utica, N. Y., April 12, 1871.

His second wife was Isabel Rogers, of New York, whom
he married in 1876. She is now (1894) residing at New
York.

THE CHILDREN AND GRANDCHILDREN OF (*132*) AUDLEY
WILLIAM AND MARY ELIZABETH VAN DEUSEN-GAZZAM.

(*252*) *Antoinette Elizabeth ;* born at Pittsburg, September 27, 1861 ; married, September 6, 1883, to John Stanley
Fredericks, of the Baltimore Bar. Of this marriage there
was issue four children :—

> (*332*) *Edwin Stanley ;* born at Carrollton, Md.,
> August 2, 1884.
> (*333*) *Florence Antoinette ;* born at Carrollton,
> Md., July 17, 1887.
> (*334*) *Thomas Emanuel ;* born at Cartersville,
> Ga., December 17, 1890.
> (*335*) *Audley William ;* born at Cartersville, Ga.,
> March 16, 1894.

(*253*) *Mary Van Deusen ;* born at Pittsburg, August 6,
1863 ; married at Bethlehem, Pa., on June 12, 1888, to the

Rev. George Abbott Hunt, of the P. E. Church. Of this marriage there was issue three children :—

> (*336*) *Rebecca Abbott;* born at Middletown, Conn., March 30, 1889.
>
> (*337*) *Martin Van Deusen;* born at Radnor, Pa., February 7, 1891.
>
> (*338*) *George Abbott;* born at Eddington, Pa., November 12, 1893.

(*254*) *Edwin Van Deusen;* born at Utica, N. Y., February 5, 1866. Studied medicine at the University of Pennsylvania ; afterward one of the staff of resident physicians, Post-Graduate Hospital, New York City. Now a practicing physician of that city.

(*255*) *Irene Gilbert;* born at Utica, N. Y., May 8, 1869; married at Philadelphia, on February 7, 1893, to Edward Hagaman Hall, of New York City.

(*256*) *Maria Florence;* born at Utica, N. Y., April 4, 1871 ; now (1894) residing at Cartersville, Ga.

THE CHILDREN OF (*132*) AUDLEY WILLIAM AND ISABEL ROGERS-GAZZAM.

(*257*) *Joseph Murphy;* born May 9, 1877.
(*258*) *Lilabel;* born February 23, 1879.
(*259*) *Emma Louise;* died in infancy.

(*133*) EMMA LOUISE GAZZAM-MACKENZIE.

Emma Louise, second child and only daughter of (*34*) Edward Despard and Elizabeth Antoinette Gazzam, was born at Pittsburg, November 4, 1837. She married in the same city, June 5, 1856, John F. Mackenzie, a talented member of the Allegheny County Bar, who during the war was secretary of the Examining Board of Paymasters, afterwards practicing law at Philadelphia for a number of years.

Emma Louise Gazzam-Mackenzie was a woman of gentle, self-sacrificing, and affectionate disposition, passing through life highly esteemed and greatly beloved by all who knew her. After several years of suffering she died at Shamokin, Northumberland County, Pa., on the 27th day of June, 1887. Her husband survived her only a few months, dying at Philadelphia, Pa., on February 28, 1888. Their remains rest in Monument Cemetery, Philadelphia.

THE CHILDREN OF JOHN F. AND (*133*) EMMA LOUISE GAZ-ZAM-MACKENZIE.

(*260*) *Edward Gazzam;* born in Pitt Township, Allegheny County, Pa., July 4, 1858. Entered the printing business at an early age, in which he continued for many years. Now (1894) connected with the Porous Waterproofing Company, of Philadelphia. Married at Philadelphia, September 8, 1881, Mary C. Welsh, of that city. Of this marriage there was issue five children, all born at Philadelphia :—

(*339*) *Adele La Roche;* born August 15, 1882.

(*340*) *Mary C.;* born and died in the month of March, 1884.

ANTOINE DeBEELEN MACKENZIE.

(See page 45.)

45

(*341*) *Frances;* born October 8, 1886.

(*342*) *Anna Gazzam;* born October 2, 1888; died in February, 1889.

(*343*) *Edward Gazzam;* born Nov. 29, 1889.

(*261*) *Franklin Irish;* born in Pitt Township, Allegheny County, Pa., July 15, 1859. Studied medicine at the Jefferson College, Philadelphia, and was one of the projectors of the Children's Sanitarium, now a prosperous and extremely beneficent institution. Died at Philadelphia, August 27, 1878, his remains resting in Monument Cemetery, Philadelphia.

(*262*) *Antoine deBeelen;* born at Pittsburg, May 29, 1861. Entered the printing business at an early age, first becoming apprentice in the office of *Taggarts' Sunday Times*, Philadelphia, where he remained until 1884, when he went to Shamokin, Pa., conducting the *Sentinel* newspaper of that town for four years, during which time he was also special correspondent for the Philadelphia *Ledger*, New York *Sun*, Boston *Globe* and Cincinnati *Enquirer*. Returning to Philadelphia he did reportorial work on the *News* and *Taggarts' Sunday Times*, of that city. On April 7, 1890, the *Evening World*, of Reading, Pa., was successfully launched upon the journalistic sea by Charles F. Haage, with Mr. Mackenzie in the editor's chair, a position he still (1894) occupies. He is a member of the Pennsylvania State Editorial Association, the Reading Press Club, and the International League of Press Clubs. He married Adeline Barger Gregg, of Philadelphia, in that city, on November 30, 1889. This union has resulted in the birth of one child :—

(*344*) *Nina deBeelen;* born at Reading, Pa., on November 17, 1890.

(*263*) *Joseph Gazzam;* born at Vineland, N. J., on November 28, 1870. Was educated at Lawrenceville (N. J.) Academy and Penn Charter School, Philadelphia, Pa., at which latter school he was president of the Penn Charter Athletic Association and of the Inter-Academic Athletic Association, winning many prizes in field sports, at which he has always been highly proficient. He was captain of the foot ball, base ball and tug-of-war teams, and editor of the *Penn Charter Magazine.* Subsequently entered the Wharton School of Finance in the University of Pennsylvania as a special student, remaining, however, only one year, passing all examinations with credit. While attending the University he was a member of the $K\Phi\Psi$ Fraternity, Iota Chapter, manager of the Track Team and athletic editor of the *University Courier.* He was recently engaged in importing laces and lace curtains, being senior partner of the firm of Mackenzie & Jenkins, of Philadelphia, Pa. Joseph Gazzam Mackenzie is fourth vice president of the Pennsylvania Club, of Philadelphia; member of the Pennsylvania Historical Society, the Philadelphia Humane Society and Skating Club, the Philadelphia Cricket Club, the Republican City Committee, and the University Republican Club, as well as a director of the North Carolina Hedge and Wire Fence Company. Married at Philadelphia, Pa., June 13, 1894, Jennie Randolph Dorsey, of that city.

(*264*) *Harold Darragh;* born at Philadelphia, February 17, 1881. At present (1894) a student at the Stewart Academy, Reading, Pa.

JOSEPH M. GAZZAM.

(See page 47.)

(134) JOSEPH MURPHY GAZZAM.

While it is true that many of the greatest names on the pages of the world's history have been won by men of obscure parentage, yet investigation will usually show that such have been especially endowed by nature with indomitable will power, robust health or other advantages, they being thus, by a combined strength of mind and body, enabled to acquire traits and habits not originally inherent. Such men necessarily mark an advance in the history of the family from which they descend.

But there are men who have gained distinction in life without the incalculable aid of strong physical condition, and in such cases one naturally looks for inherited mental capacity, the individual's ability predicating the merit of those from whom he has sprung.

Joseph Murphy Gazzam, the subject of this sketch, may with propriety be classed among the latter. Descended from parents of cultivation and refinement, it is to be expected that he should have always evinced a desire for similar culture, and, despite almost continuous ill-health, it is not singular that he should have acquired distinction in his professional, political and social career.

He was born in the city of Pittsburg, December 2, 1842, being the second son and third child of (34) Dr. Edward Despard and Elizabeth Antoinette deBeelen-Gazzam. The first fourteen years of Mr. Gazzam's life differed somewhat from the ordinary, owing to lack of robust health, his parents considering it advisable to keep him from the ardors and restraints of regular school life. At home, however, under the careful tuition of his father, he gained the rudimentary elements of education, so that he was not by any means deficient when, at this age, he entered the Western University of Pennsylvania. Here he remained for three and a half years, at the end of which time his health compelled a temporary suspension of study. An extended tour throughout the Western States greatly benefitted him, however, so that when he returned he felt capable of beginning what afterwards proved an earnest and exhaustive study of the law. On January 4, 1861, he entered the office of David Reed, Esq., and three years later, January 6, 1864, he was admitted to the Allegheny County Bar. In a short time his practice became so extensive that he was able to decline all criminal cases save those of regular clients, this, too, in face of the fact that he had made quite a reputation in this branch of the profession, although the practice was always distasteful to him. In November, 1867, he was admitted to the Supreme Court of Pennsylvania ; in May, 1869, to the Circuit and District Courts of the United States, and March 19, 1870, upon motion of the late Hon. Benjamin F. Butler, of Massachusetts, to the Supreme Court of the United States. In the latter body he was remarked as one of the youngest members ever admitted to practice before it.

In 1871 he was elected a director for Pennsylvania in the United States Law Association, and in 1872 he entered into a law partnership with Hon. Alexander G. Cochran. The firm of Gazzam & Cochran became widely known throughout the United States, and was continued until 1879, when, owing to the removal of Mr. Cochran to St. Louis, it was dissolved.

Mr. Gazzam's life at this period had become a very busy one. He was solicitor for a number of leading corporations of Pittsburg, among them being the City Bank, the Security Trust Company, the Iron City Fire Insurance Company, and others, besides being president of the United States Building and Loan Association. Despite this extremely active professional career, Mr. Gazzam found time to take a leading part in numerous social organizations, being president of the Pittsburg Gymnastic Association, president of the Hygeia Base Ball Club, as well as an officer, or officer and director, in many other similar organizations.

A fondness for the political arena is one of the characteristics undoubtedly inherited by Mr. Gazzam. In early life it induced him to take active part in the municipal government of his native city. He was frequently called upon to speak at political meetings in various campaigns, and his decisive and practical expressions advocating many needed reforms soon attracted general attention. In consequence he became (in 1869) Republican candidate to represent the First Ward of Pittsburg in City Councils. Being elected he was subsequently enabled to carry many of these excellent ideas into effect, and to show himself a capable and patriotic public official. His name at this time was prominently mentioned in connection with the Select Branch of Councils, and also for the Mayoralty. Concerning the former the Pittsburg *Sunday Times*, of November 10, 1872, said :—

If strict attention to every duty and unceasing devotion to the best interests of the city are commendable in a public officer, then Mr. Gazzam will certainly be rewarded with a seat in the Select Branch of our City Legislature. During the year about to close Mr. Gazzam has been prominent in all important legislation, and has ever been on the popular side. His constituents will do themselves a good service by honoring Mr. Gazzam with promotion.

Alluding to the nomination for the Mayoralty, the Pittsburg *Evening Bulletin*, of May 9, 1872, said :—

Among the names suggested for the Mayoralty is that of Joseph M. Gazzam. Mr. Gazzam is a young man of ability. He has represented the First Ward in the Common Council for several years, and the people have the utmost confidence in his honesty and integrity.

An important step in the career of Mr. Gazzam occurred in 1876, when, by acclamation of the nominating convention, he became Republican candidate for the Forty-third Senatorial District. He was elected by a large majority. As a member of the Senate he soon ranked as of the highest ability and character. Fair-minded yet tenacious, pacific yet thoroughly equipped for debate, he formed his opinions on public measures with deliberation and candor, and defended them with courage and skill. He was a zealous worker for Republican principles, though utterly devoid of all that savored of "offensive partisanship," and so wise were his counsels that at the expiration of his term he had gained a most enviable position in his party. One of the bills introduced by Mr. Gazzam was for a marriage license law (similar to that now in effect in Pennsylvania), which was then defeated.

In 1882 he was prominently mentioned throughout the State as a candidate for the Lieutenant-Governorship. This was at a time, however, when private reasons urged Mr. Gazzam to discourage all efforts made in his behalf by a legion of friends, and so his name was not presented at the convention. The following extract from an editorial in the Philadelphia *News*, published at the time, will convey an idea of the general esteem in which his political actions are held :—

There are many names being brought forward for the Lieutenant-Governorship of this State. The *Press* of this city refers as follows to the subject : "Various journals of the State have presented the name of ex-Senator Joseph M. Gazzam as candidate for Lieutenant-Governor on the

Republican ticket. Mr. Gazzam has made an honorable record in public life. He was the author of the law which prevented a session of the Legislature in 1880, thus making a large saving for the State. He is recommended as affable and well versed in parliamentary law and having the qualities to make a strong candidate if nominated." This complimentary notice is well deserved. Mr. Gazzam stands the peer of any man in the State in purity of character, fullness of culture and clearness of intellect. Having had years of experience in the State Senate, he is fully qualified to perform any service required of the Lieutenant-Governor. And as the term of Governor has been extended to four years, all the uncertainties which attach to a Presidential term attaches to it. Therefore, whoever may be selected as candidate for Lieutenant-Governor should be qualified, in the event of need, to act as Governor. This Mr. Gazzam is amply qualified to do. Prudent, cautious, and with good judgment, he would fill the Executive chair with ability and success. If the policy this year shall be to make up a ticket so unexceptionable that all Republicans will be glad to support it, no better name can be selected for Lieutenant-Governor. And this is the policy which should obtain. Locality this year should give place to quality in candidates. It is the one thing that is important above all else. And if this policy shall prevail, Mr. Gazzam will be in the front for the Lieutenant-Governorship.

Unfortunately the policy above indicated did not prevail in the convention that followed. A slated ticket was rushed through, which proved so distasteful to the Independent Republicans throughout the State that they met in convention and put a ticket of their own in the field, the final outcome being the defeat of both Republican tickets and the election of the regular Democratic nominees.

Senator Gazzam moved from his native city to Philadelphia in 1879. Upon this occasion all the Pittsburg papers commented upon his removal in the most flattering terms. The *Critic* said :—

Pittsburg's loss is Philadelphia's gain. The community has long since learned to respect and esteem him for his manly qualities, his genial disposition, his inborn courtesy, his strict integrity, his usefulness in public life and his devotion to all that Pittsburgers regard as noblest and dearest.

After his arrival in Philadelphia Mr. Gazzam opened an office at 714 Walnut street, his law practice increasing rapidly. Upon the completion of the Girard Building, at Broad and Chestnut streets, Mr. Gazzam removed his offices to it, engaging six commodious rooms, which he furnished luxuriously as business offices. Recently, however, he has not actively practiced, owing to the pressing duties of the numerous offices filled by him in various corporations, and his connection with sundry other business enterprises. He was one of the projectors of the Beech Creek, Clearfield & Southwestern Railroad (later known as the Beech Creek), a railroad which, beginning at Jersey Shore, Pa., had its terminus in the thriving borough of Gazzam, named after the subject of this sketch.

At the present time (1894) Mr. Gazzam is president of the Philadelphia Finance Company, and the Bridgewater Cordage Company (Philadelphia); of the Kenilworth Inn Company, and Kenilworth Land Company (Asheville, N. C.); of the Etowah Iron Company (Georgia), and of the Wilkesbarre and Western Railroad Company (Pennsylvania). He is vice president of the Quaker City National Bank (Philadelphia); of the Ames-Bonner Brush Company (Toledo, Ohio); Auer Light Company (South America); Central Coal and Coke Company and Dent's Run Coke Company (Pennsylvania). He is a director in the Spring Garden Insurance Company (Philadelphia), the Delaware Company, and eight other corporations, making a total of twenty-nine corporations in which he is concerned either as an officer or director.

With all his arduous business duties, however, Mr. Gazzam, owing to his methodical habits, still finds time to devote to literary and other pursuits. He is a life member of the Pennsylvania Historical Society, the Fairmount Park

MRS. JOSEPH M. GAZZAM.
(Nee Nellie May Andrews.)
(See Page 53.)

Art Association, and of the Pennsylvania Horticultural Society. He is also a member of the Pennsylvania Club, one of the leading political organizations of the State, of which he was for three years president, declining nomination for a fourth term recently tendered him. He is also a member of the Union League Club, of Philadelphia, and of the Citizens' Municipal Association, of the Philadelphia Cricket Club, of the Lawyers' Club, of the Germantown Cricket Club, of Philadelphia ; the Pennsylvania Society for the Prevention of Cruelty to Animals, the Geneological Society of Pennsylvania, University Archæological Association, the American Academy of Political and Social Science, and the Pennsylvania Fish Protective Association, of which latter he filled the office of president recently.

Mr. Gazzam married, October 30, 1878, Anna, daughter of the late John G. Reading, one of Pennsylvania's successful business men, and a great-grandson of Hon. John Reading, Colonial Governor of New Jersey. Two children were the result of this union :—

(*265*) *Sada ;* born September 1, 1879 ; died November 17, 1880.

(*266*) *Antoinette Elizabeth ;* born March 8, 1883.

Mr. Gazzam married a second time September 7, 1893, Nellie May, daughter of Benjamin and Olivia A. Andrews, of New Orleans, who still survives (1894).

1515

[From a picture in the possession of A. deB. Mackenzie, Reading, Pa.]

BARON DeBEELEN BERTHOLFF.
(See page 57.)

BIOGRAPHICAL SKETCH

OF THE

DeBEELEN FAMILY.

(AMERICAN BRANCH.)

THE DeBEELEN FAMILY.

When the Revolution that resulted in the freedom of the American Colonies was over, and after peace had been declared between the United States and Great Britain, Joseph II, Emperor of Austria, sent as Resident Minister of that country to the new republic, (*1*) Baron Frederic Eugene Francois deBeelen Bertholff.*

The Baron brought with him his wife, the Baroness deBeelen (*nee* Marie Theresa de Castro y Toledo), and their only son, (*2*) Constantine Antoine, and remained as Minister from 1783 to 1787. During the latter year he was ordered home ; but, being prevented from returning by reason of political complications, his estates in Austria were seized by the Government and confiscated. It was this, probably, which finally determined the Baron to remain in America, and leaving Philadelphia he settled in Chester County, Pa., near what is now Honeybrook Station, where he built an imposing residence, for a long time known as "The Castle," the surrounding estate lying partly in Chester and partly in Lancaster Counties. Later the Baron removed to York County, where he acquired some considerable additional property.†

Baron deBeelen Bertholff and his wife both died in York County, Pa., and their remains repose in a sequestered cemetery upon the bank of the Conawaga, the spot marked by what was once an imposing monument.

---

*For information concerning the earlier family see "Annuaire de la Noblesse de Belgique," published by Baron Isidore de Stein D'Altenstein, Belgium, 1871. Also, see "Denny's Memoirs of his Father." Also, Rev. Lambrig's " History of the Catholic Church."

†See deed, post.

(2) CONSTANTINE ANTOINE DeBEELEN.

Constantine Antoine, the only child of (1) Baron and Baroness deBeelen Bertholff, was born at Brussels, Belgium, June 9, 1770.

An ancient document in Latin, on hand-made paper much worn by the tooth of time, bears the following endorsement in English, in the firm and cultivated handwriting of Constantine Antoine deBeelen :—

My Father's Certificate of my Baptism (Mon Baptistaire), taken from the record of the Cathedral of Ste. Gudule in the City of Bruxelles, in Belgium.

The contents of this paper, translated, are as follows :

On the ninth of June, in the year 1770, was baptized Constantine Antoine, legitimate son of Sir Frederic Eugene Francois deBeelen Bertholff and Lady Jeanne Marie Theresa de Castro y Toledo, husband and wife ; born at nine o'clock in the morning, the 9th day of June, 1770. The sponsors were by name Lady Marie Theresa Constance deBeelen and Sir Antoine de Castro y Toledo, Toparcka in Zoombeeck, Vandengver ; and Lady Carolina and Sir Nicholas deBeelen, husband and wife.*

After the death of his parents (2) Constantine Antoine deBeelen Bertholff settled in Pittsburg, where he became well and favorably known as an importing merchant. It is said that had he so desired he could have returned to the home of his ancestors, reclaiming the title and estates of his father. But it appears he had become too much imbued with the love of American institutions to submit himself and his fortunes to monarchical rule.

---

*The certificate of baptism is (1894) in the possession of Hon. Joseph M. Gazzam, of Philadelphia, Pa.

CONSTANTINE ANTOINE DeBEELEN.

(See page 58.)

While in Pittsburg he discontinued the use of the suffix Bertholff, being commonly known as Antoine deBeelen.

He married in that city Elizabeth Antoinette Murphy, daughter and only child of Captain Patrick Murphy, of the Continental Army, around whose parentage there clings a little romance.

It seems that sometime during the latter half of the 17th century, a poor gentleman became tutor in the family of an Irish nobleman, the father of a beautiful daughter. The tutor fell in love with his charge, there was an elopement, a hasty marriage, and—America.

During the Revolution the tutor became an officer in the Continental Army. After peace was declared he moved to Pittsburg, in which city his wife died at the time of the birth of her daughter. It was this daughter who became the wife of Antoine deBeelen.

Upon the death of his wife Captain Murphy sent to Carlisle, Pa., for a young woman named Molly, who had left Ireland to come to America as maid to Mrs. Murphy, marrying here and settling at Carlisle, shortly afterward becoming a widow. She consented to take charge of the infant daughter, and subsequently Captain Murphy married her. From this union there was no issue, but Mrs. Murphy survived the death of the Captain many years. He left her comparatively well off and she became projector of many business enterprises, being interested in the first gas works and one of the first rolling mills ever started in Pittsburg. Through clear-headed business ability she acquired considerable additional property, in later years extremely valuable.

Dying childless, this property was bequeathed to the descendants of her stepdaughter, Elizabeth Antoinette.

Constantine Antoine deBeelen and Elizabeth Antoinette, his wife, left several children. But two of them married, however :—

(*3*) *Mary;* married Dr. William Simpson, of Pittsburg, Pa., and was the mother of the wife of the late Benjamin Rush, Esq., of Philadelphia.

(*4*) *Elizabeth Antoinette;* born at Pittsburg, Pa., in 1817; married, March 24, 1835, to Dr. Edward D. Gazzam.* Mrs. E. A. Gazzam was a gentlewoman of fine education, of polished and easy manners, hospitable disposition, good and truly charitable nature, and ever ambitious to relieve the wants of her suffering fellow-beings—a liberal Christian in the broadest sense of the word. She lived a life of influence, and in her death, which occurred suddenly on the 25th of July, 1871, at Pittsburg, all who knew her recognized the transition of an immortal soul from earth to a happy and eternal heaven.

Constantine Antoine deBeelen survived his first wife, and subsequently married a Miss Aiken. Of this marriage there was issue five children :—

(*5*) *Eliza;* born March 24, 1816.

(*6*) *Frederick A.;* born April 12, 1827 ; married and lived in Brazil for a number of years.

(*7*) *Anna Maria;* married to General James A. Oakes, U. S. A., in November, 1854.

(*8*) *Caroline;* married to George S. Lovett, of Philadelphia, in October, 1850.

(*9*) *Adeline;* married to Colonel W. Milnor Roberts, a celebrated civil engineer, who for many years was in the service of Dom Pedro, the late Emperor of Brazil.

√

---

*See page 40.

[From a picture in the possession of J. M. Gazzam, Philadelphia, Pa.]

MRS. EDWARD D. GAZZAM
(Nee Elizabeth Antoinette deBeelen.)

(See page 60.)

INTERESTING OLD DOCUMENTS.

There are several old documents in existence that pertain to the Baron deBeelen's residence in this country. The following is the copy of a deed relating to the purchase by him of a tract of land in York county, Pa., which is of immediate interest :—

THIS INDENTURE, Made the first day of February, in the year of our Lord, one thousand seven hundred and ninety-eight, between John Brillinger, of York Township, in the County of York and State of Pennsylvania, miller, and Catharine, his wife, of the one part, and Frederic Eugene Francois, Baron deBeelen Bertholff, of Manchester Township, in the County of York aforesaid, gentleman, of the other part.

WITNESSETH, That the said John Brillinger, and Catharine, his wife, for and in consideration of the sum of two hundred and fifty pounds of the current gold and silver money of Pennsylvania, to him, the said John Brillinger, in hand paid by the said Frederic Eugene Francois, Baron deBeelen Bertholff, at and before the ensealing and delivery of these presents, the receipt and payment whereof is hereby acknowledged, and the said Frederic Eugene Francois, Baron deBeelen Bertholff, thereof acquitted and forever discharged by these presents.

Have granted, bargained, sold in fee, offered, released and confirmed, and by these presents do grant, b argain, sell in fee, offer, release and confirm unto the said Frederic Eugene Francois, Baron deBeelen Bertholff, and to his heirs and assigns, all that the following described messuage, tenement and tract of land, which is situate, lying and being

in Hellam Township, in the County of York aforesaid,
bounded and limited as follows : Beginning at a marked
black oak; thence by land of Peter Garhaw, Sr., formerly, now
of John Fritz, north sixty-five degrees, east one hundred and
thirty-six perches, to a marked chestnut oak ; thence by
lands of James Smith, Esq., formerly, now of Wilkes Kettera and Samuel Jago, Esq., north fifty-five degrees, east
one hundred and eighty-three perches, to a marked white
oak, thence north twenty-three degrees, west seventeen
perches, to a marked black oak ; thence by land of Wilkes
Kettera and Samuel Jago, south seventy degrees, west one
hundred and six perches, to a marked chestnut; thence north
thirty degrees, west forty perches, to a marked chestnut oak;
thence by vacant land, south sixty-two degrees, west seventy-
two perches, to a marked chestnut oak; south thirty degrees,
east twelve perches, to a marked hickory; thence by the
said vacant lands of Philip Fellero, south sixty degrees, west
one hundred and fifty-seven perches, to stones ; thence by
lands of John Fritz, south forty degrees, east seventy-nine
perches, to the place of beginning, containing 134 acres, and
the usual allowance of six acres to the hundred for roads, &c.,
within the bounds and limits thereof. [Being the same
which Philip Klug and Christina, his wife, by indenture of
bargain and sale bearing date the 23d day of January last past
for the consideration therein mentioned, did grant and confirm unto the said John Brillinger (party hereto), and to his
heirs and assigns forever, as, in and by the said in part
recited deed, intended to be recorded, reference having
thereunto had, may more fully and at large appear.]

TOGETHER with all and singular the houses, out-houses,
edifices and buildings thereon erected and built, and all
ways, woods, under woods, waters, water courses, meadows,
orchards, gardens, profits, commodities, advantages, emolu-

ments, hereditaments and appurtenances whatsoever to the said described messuage, tenements and tract of land belonging, or in anywise appertaining, and the reversions, reminders, rents, issues and profits thereof, also all the estate right, title, interest, use, possession, property claim and demand whatsoever of them, the said John Brillinger, and Catharine, his wife, in law or equity or otherwise howsoever, of, into or out of the said described piece, or parcel of land, or any part thereof; together, also, with all such deeds or true copies of deeds, evidences and writings touching and concerning the hereby granted premises, or any part or parcel thereof, to be had and taken at the costs and charges of the said Frederic Eugene Francois, Baron deBeelen Bertholff, his heirs and assigns, to have and to hold the said described messuage, tenement and tract of land containing one hundred and thirty-four acres, and the usual allowance, as the same is above described, and the premises hereby granted, mentioned or intended so to be, with the appurtenances, unto the aforesaid Frederic Eugene Francois, Baron deBeelen Bertholff, his heirs and assigns, to the only proper use, benefit and behoof of the said Frederic Eugene Francois, Baron deBeelen Bertholff, his heirs and assigns forever, under and subject to the residue of the purchase money, interest and quit rents (if any) due, and to become due, and payable to such person, or persons, appointed to receive the same; and the said John Brillinger, for himself and for Catharine, his wife, and their heirs, doth covenant, promise and grant to and with the said Frederic Eugene Francois, Baron deBeelen Bertholff, his heirs and assigns, by these presents, that he, the said John Brillinger, and his heirs, the said described messuage, tenement and tract of land hereby bargained and sold with the appurtenances unto the said Frederic Eugene Francois, Baron deBeelen

Bertholff, his heirs and assigns, against him, the said John Brillinger and Catharine, his wife, and their heirs, and against the heirs of Charles King, and all and every other person or persons whomsoever, lawfully claiming, or to claim, the same, or any part thereof, by, from, or under him, or them, or any or either of them, shall and will warrant and forever defend.

IN WITNESS WHEREOF, The said John Brillinger and Catharine, his wife, to these presents hath hereunto set their hands and seals, dated on the day and year first and within written.

JOHN BRILLINGER,   (SEAL)

Her
CATHARINE ✕ BRILLINGER.   (SEAL)
Mark.

Sealed and delivered in presence of

CHR. SINN,
GEO. LEWIS LEFLER.

Received on the date of the foregoing indenture from the within-named Frederick Eugene Francois, Baron deBeelen Bertholff, the sum of two hundred and fifty pounds, current money of Pennsylvania, in full of the consideration money within mentioned.

JOHN BRILLINGER.

Witness present :

CHR. SINN.

YORK COUNTY ss :

Before me, the subscriber, one of the justices of the peace, for said county, personally appeared John Brillinger and

Catharine, his wife, the grantors in the foregoing indenture, named and acknowledged the same to be their act and deed to the intent that it may be recorded as such according to law. She, the said Catharine, being of full age and by me privately examined, declares that she became a party thereto without coercion or compulsion from her said husband, the contents thereof being first made known unto her, freely consented.

In testimony whereof I have hereunto set my hand and seal this first day of February, in the year of our Lord, one thousand seven hundred and ninety-eight.

GEO. LEWIS LEFLER.

A true copy taken from and compared with the original at York the third day of February, A. D., 1798.

F. BARNITZ, Recorder.

SERVICES BY INDENTURE.

The original of the following indenture, faded, weather-stained and well-worn, is at present in the possession of Hon. Joseph M. Gazzam, of Philadelphia, being of particular interest at this time on account of the obsolete custom to which it relates :—

THIS INDENTURE, made this twenty-sixth day of February, in the year of our Lord one thousand seven hundred eighty-four, WITNESSETH that I, Philip Michel, and Elizabeth, his wife, of Robeson township, in the county of Berks, and State of Pennsylvania, do bind our son, Amos Michel, unto Frederick Spar, of Brecknock township, county and State aforesaid, to him, his heirs, or assigns. The said Amos Michel is to continue and serve from the fifteenth day of March, ensuing the date hereof, until the full end and term of seventeen years, to be ended and fully completed, during all which term the said servant his master true and faithfully shall serve and keep his lawful commands gladly. Neither shall he do damage to the said master, nor see it done by others, without telling or giving notice to his said master. He shall not waste his master's goods, nor lend them to any without his consent. He shall not play at cards, dice, or any unlawful game whereby his master may be damaged, with his own goods or the goods of others. He shall not commit fornication, nor contract matrimony. He shall not absent himself at any time from the service of his master, nor haunt ale houses or taverns; but in all ways behave himself like a true and faithful servant. And said master shall procure and provide for him sufficient meat, drink and apparel, washing and lodging, during the above term; also the said master shall give him eight months' schooling, but not till he is nine years old, and two suits of clothes, the one for his freedom suit of clothes that is sufficient; one axe, and one grubbing hoe, one pair of mall rings and two iron wedges. And for the true performance of the said covenant and agreement, according to the true intent and meaning thereof, both the said parties bindeth themselves unto the other firmly by these presents.

IN WITNESS WHEREOF, They have hereunto set their hands and seals the day and year above written.

His
PHILIP ⋈ MICHEL.　　　(SEAL)
Mark.

Her
ELIZABETH ⋈ MICHEL.　　(SEAL)
Mark.

Done before me, February 26, 1784.

JACOB MORGAN.

In consideration of the sum of seven shillings and six-pence, Margaret Spar, on November 5, 1784, assigned the time of Amos Michel (referred to in the foregoing indenture) to John Evans. For seven pounds young Michel's services were assigned by John Evans to Joseph Ashton, January 14, 1792. Joseph Ashton for nine pounds assigned to Frederick Spar, May 29, 1792. Frederick Spar for eighteen pounds assigned to Baron de Beelen Bertholff, March 7, 1794. The Baron for nineteen pounds, ten shillings, assigned to James Hamilton, March 17, 1795. James Hamilton for eighteen pounds, fifteen shillings, assigned to John Bicking, July 21, 1799. The last assignment of Michel's services was made by John Bicking to James Hamilton, September 4, 1800, the sum paid being three pounds, fifteen shillings.

The following is a copy of the transfer of the services of Amos Michel, made by the Baron deBeelen Bertholff, together with a *fac simile* of the Baron's signature :—

IN CONSIDERATION of the sum of nineteen pounds, ten shillings, current money of Pennsylvania, to me in hand paid this day by Mr. James Hamilton, I do assign the within-mentioned servant's time to said James Hamilton, to serve him, his heirs, or assigns the remainder of his time, as witnesseth my hand and seal this seventeenth day of March, 1795.

DESCENDANTS OF WILLIAM GAZZAM I.

WHOSE NAMES APPEAR IN THIS WORK.

[NOTE.—The numbers on the extreme outside show parentage; those in parenthesis (   ) at the end of the names, children.]

---

1 Gazzam, William (2-9)

1- 2 Gazzam, Martha (10-15)
3 Gazzam, Mary (16-24)
4 Gazzam, Sarah
5 Gazzam, William (25-40)
6 Gazzam, Lydia (41-49)
7 Gazzam, Joseph (50-56)
8 Gazzam, Rebecca (57-63)
9 Gazzam, Mary Alice (64-74)

2- 10 Girlling, Martha Maria
11 Girlling, Elizabeth
12 Girlling, Sarah (75-77)
13 Girlling, Rebecca
14 Girlling, Mary
15 Girlling, Thomas L. (78)

3- 16 Larwill, Joseph H.
17 Larwill, Julia Robinson
18 Larwill, William (79-87)
19 Larwill, Mary ⎫ Twins
20 Larwill, Benoni ⎭
21 Larwill, Mary B.
22 Larwill, John (88-94)
23 Larwill, Ebenezer
24 Larwill, Jabez B. (95-103)

5- 25 Gazzam, William
26 Gazzam, Anna (104-107)
27 Gazzam, Elizabeth
28 Gazzam, Sarah

5- 29 Gazzam, Jos. P. (108-109)
30 Gazzam, Chas. W.(110-120)
31 Gazzam, Cath.Sel.(121-130)
32 Gazzam, Louise P.
33 Gazzam, Audley H. (131)
34 Gazzam, Edw. D. (132-134)
35 Gazzam, Mary A. (135-140)
36 Gazzam, Ebenezer (141-154)
37 Gazzam, (Infant.)
38 Gazzam, (Infant.)
39 Gazzam, (Infant.)
40 Gazzam, (Infant.)

6- 41 Kimpton, William G.
42 Kimpton, David
43 Kimpton, Joseph
44 Kimpton, David
45 Kimpton, Lydia
46 Kimpton, Mary
47 Kimpton, Rebecca
48 Kimpton, Joshua
49 Kimpton, Mary Alice

7- 50 Gazzam, Emma Goodcheap
51 Gazzam, James
52 Gazzam, Ann
53 Gazzam, Joseph
54 Gazzam, Susannah
55 Gazzam, Sarah
56 Gazzam, Thos. Goodcheap

8– 57 Jones, Rebecca Gazzam
    58 Jones, Edward Oldfield
    59 Jones, Charles
    60 Jones, Emma Goodcheap
    61 Jones, Martha E.
    62 Jones, Anna Selina
    63 Jones, Mary Alice

9– 64 Taylor, William Gazzam
    65 Taylor, Thomas Davis
    66 Taylor, Thomas William
    67 Taylor, Benj. C. (155-158)
    68 Taylor, Othniel H.(159-162)
    69 Taylor, Mary A. (163-167)
    70 Taylor, Sarah Fulton
    71 Taylor, Martha (168-180)
    72 Taylor, Wm. Rivers
    73 Taylor, Isaac E. (181-184)
    74 Taylor, Joseph G. (185-191)

12– 75 Watson, Wm. Lansdell
    76 Watson, James
    77 Watson, George Robinson

15– 78 Girlling, William

18– 79 Larwill, Julia M.
    80 Larwill, Mary G.
    81 Larwill, John C.
    82 Larwill, Levinia
    83 Larwill, Elizabeth C.
    84 Larwill, Lucretia
    85 Larwill, William
    86 Larwill, Joseph IJ.
    87 Larwill, Oscar

22– 88 Larwill, William G.
    89 Larwill, Ann E.
    90 Larwill, Martha H.
    91 Larwill, Emma M.
    92 Larwill, John S.
    93 Larwill, Julia F.
    94 Larwill, (Infant son)

24– 95 Larwill, Joseph H.
    96 Larwill, Mary G.
    97 Larwill, Julia C.

24– 98 Larwill, William J.
    99 Larwill, John Fawcett
    100 Larwill, Nancy Quinby
    101 Larwill, George M.
    102 Larwill, Amanda J.
    103 Larwill, Leroy J.

26–104 Bucknall, Joanna Rooker
    105 Bucknall, Ebenezer G.
    106 Bucknall, S. R. (192-193)
    107 Bucknall, Martha E.

29–108 Gazzam, James B. (194)
    109 Gazzam, Harriet Breading

30–110 Gazzam, Catharine Selina
    111 Gazzam, Audley Hart
    112 Gazzam, George Gano (195)
    113 Gazzam, } Twin sons
    114 Gazzam, {
    115 Gazzam, C. W. (196-201)
    116 Gazzam, Clement Lea
    117 Gazzam, William Parker
    118 Gazzam, Henry McC. (202)
    119 Gazzam, Claudius Douglas
    120 Gazzam, John Lea

31–121 Butler, Chas. J. (203-207)
    122 Butler, Jos. C. (208-216)
    123 Butler, Frances (217-220)
    124 Butler, Harriet (221-229)
    125 Butler, Sarah P. (230)
    126 Butler, Kate Aurelia
    127 Butler, Richard (231-234)
    128 Butler, Caroline (235-239)
    129 Butler, John G. (240-245)
    130 Butler, Alice O. (246-249)

33–131 Gazzam, Marg. (250-251)

34–132 Gazzam, Audley (252-259)
    133 Gazzam, Emma (260-264)
    134 Gazzam, Jos. M. (265-266)

35–135 Butler, Clementina G.
    136 Butler, Frederick Tomlin
    137 Butler, Elizabeth O.

123-217 Walter, Jos G. (320-322)
    218 Walter, Selina Louisa
    219 Walter, Sarah Loomis
    220 Walter, Augusta (323-324)

124-221 McMillan, Cath. (325-326)
    222 McMillan, John Butler
    223 McMillan, Austin Loomis
    224 McMillan, Anna (327-329)
    225 McMillan, Joseph Butler
    226 McMillan, Jessie Garmily
    227 McMillan, Albert Walter
    228 McMillan, Thos. Erskine
    229 McMillan, Sam'l Benedick

125-230 Loomis, Austin Butler

127-231 Butler, Lina L. (330-331)
    232 Butler, Ormond
    233 Butler, Caroline Day
    234 Butler, Audley Richard

128-235 Day, Gordon Butler
    236 Day, David Henry
    237 Day, Charles Butler
    238 Day, Alice
    239 Day, Lillian Warnick

129-240 Butler, Mary Warnick
    241 Butler, Lawrence Parker
    242 Butler, Harriet McMillan
    243 Butler, Rodman
    244 Butler, Rollins
    245 Butler, Lillie

130-246 Tilden, Laura May
    247 Tilden, Charles Joseph
    248 Tilden, Alice Foster
    249 Tilden, Edith Selina

131-250 Stow, Audley Hart
    251 Stow, Edith

132-252 Gazzam, A. E. (332-335)
    253 Gazzam, Mary (336-338)
    254 Gazzam, Edwin Van D.
    255 Gazzam, Irene Gilbert
    256 Gazzam, Maria Florence

132-257 Gazzam, Joseph Murphy
    258 Gazzam, Lilabel
    259 Gazzam, Emma Louise

133-260 Mackenzie, E. G. (339-343)
    261 Mackenzie, Franklin Irish
    262 Mackenzie, A. deB. (344)
    263 Mackenzie, Jos. Gazzam
    264 Mackenzie, H. Darragh

134-265 Gazzam, Sada
    266 Gazzam, Antoinette E.

138-267 Butler, Ellis P.
    268 Butler, Adela V.
    369 Butler, George O.
    270 Butler, Alice
    271 Butler, Lawrence L.
    272 Butler, Elizabeth L.
    273 Butler, Frederick Daut
    274 Butler, Edith O.

142-275 Workman, E. (345-347)
    276 Workman, John (348-351)
    277 Workman, Amanda
    278 Workman, Ross (352-354)
    279 Workman, Selina (355-358)
    280 Workman, Harriet
    281 Workman, Henrietta
    282 Workman, Frank

146-283 Gazzam, Elizabeth A. —
    284 Gazzam, Annie A.
    285 Gazzam, May
    286 Gazzam, Letitia

147-287 Gazzam, Florence

151-288 Gazzam, Audley
    289 Gazzam, Clara
    290 Gazzam, Elizabeth
    291 Gazzam, Henry Parker
    292 Gazzam, John Harris

152-293 Gazzam, Nellie B.
    294 Gazzam, Mary
    295 Gazzam, Frank

156-296 Van Alen, Henry

157-297 Taylor, Van Campen
 298 Taylor, Southerland
 299 Taylor, William
 300 Taylor, Livingston

158-301 Taylor, Bertha

161-302 Taylor, Clarence Wills
 303 Taylor, Evelina
 304 Taylor, Annie

162-305 Taylor, Henry Genet
 306 Taylor, Richard Cooper
 307 Taylor, Helen Elizabeth

192-308 Bucknell, Nellie Lydia
 309 Bucknell, Samuel Kazlett
 310 Bucknell, Martha E.
 311 Bucknell, Marion Augusta
 312 Bucknell, Anna Maria

193-313 Bucknell, George Gordon
 314 Bucknell, Mary Russell
 315 Bucknell, Lydia Eastlack

196-316 Gazzam, Lea
 317 Gazzam,

198-318 Fisken, Keith Gazzam
 319 Fisken, Archibald Donald

217-320 Walter, Helen
 321 Walter, Alexander Dean
 322 Walter, Albert Gustav

220-323 Wallace, Selina Gazzam
 324 Wallace, Albert Walter

221-325 Beals, Walter Burgess
 326 Beals, James Burrie

224-327 Shepard, David Chauncey
 328 Shepard, Samuel McMillan
 329 Shepard, Roger Bulkley

231-330 Moore, Grace
 331 Moore, Alice

252-332 Fredericks, Edwin S.
 333 Fredericks, Florence A.
 334 Fredericks, Thomas E.
 335 Fredericks, Audley W.

253-336 Hunt, Rebecca Abbott
 337 Hunt, Martin Van Deusen
 338 Hunt, George Abbott

260-339 Mackenzie, Adele LaR.
 340 Mackenzie, Mary C.
 341 Mackenzie, Frances
 342 Mackenzie, Anna Gazzam
 343 Mackenzie, Edward G.

262-344 Mackenzie, Nina deBeelen

275-345 Newman, Charles F.
 346 Newman, John R.
 347 Newman, Jessie

276-348 Workman, Myrtle
 349 Workman, Gertrude
 350 Workman, Selina
 351 Workman, Arden

278-352 Workman, Goldie
 353 Workman, Earl Gazzam
 354 Workman, Pearl

279-355 Cobbs, Mary
 356 Cobbs, Chester
 357 Cobbs, Luther
 358 Cobbs,

FAMILY RECORD AND GENEALOGY.

(SUPPLEMENTARY.)

FAMILY RECORD AND GENEALOGY.

75

FAMILY RECORD AND GENEALOGY.

FAMILY RECORD AND GENEALOGY.

BILTMORE, N C._____1909

www.ingramcontent.com/pod-product-compliance
Lightning Source LLC
Chambersburg PA
CBHW030541270326
41927CB00008B/1464